I0409769

For Every Kid Worldwide Who Loves Coloring-

A Book By

INNOVATIVE DESIGN FOR EVERY NEED
KF
LOGOS AND BRANDING

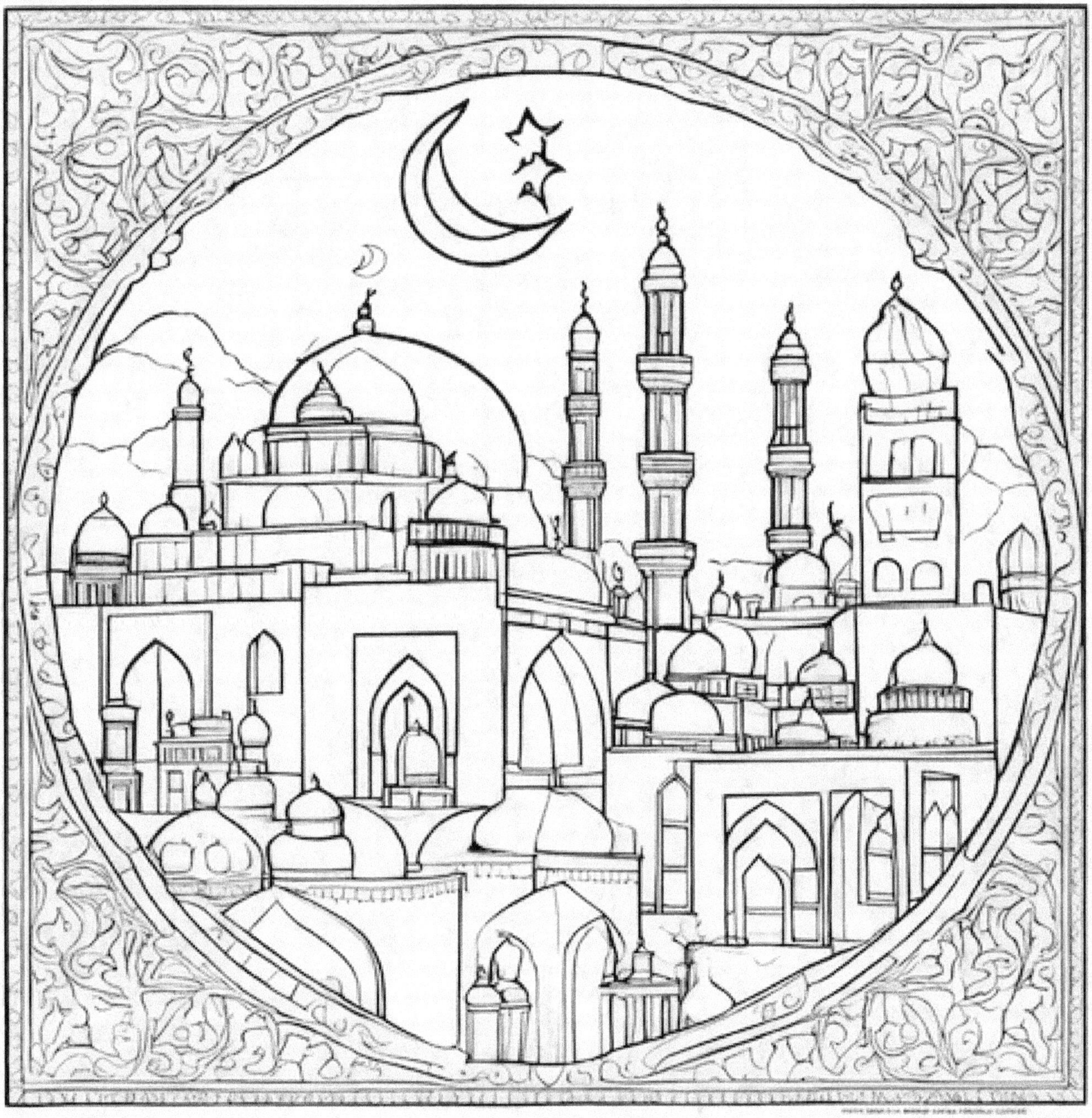

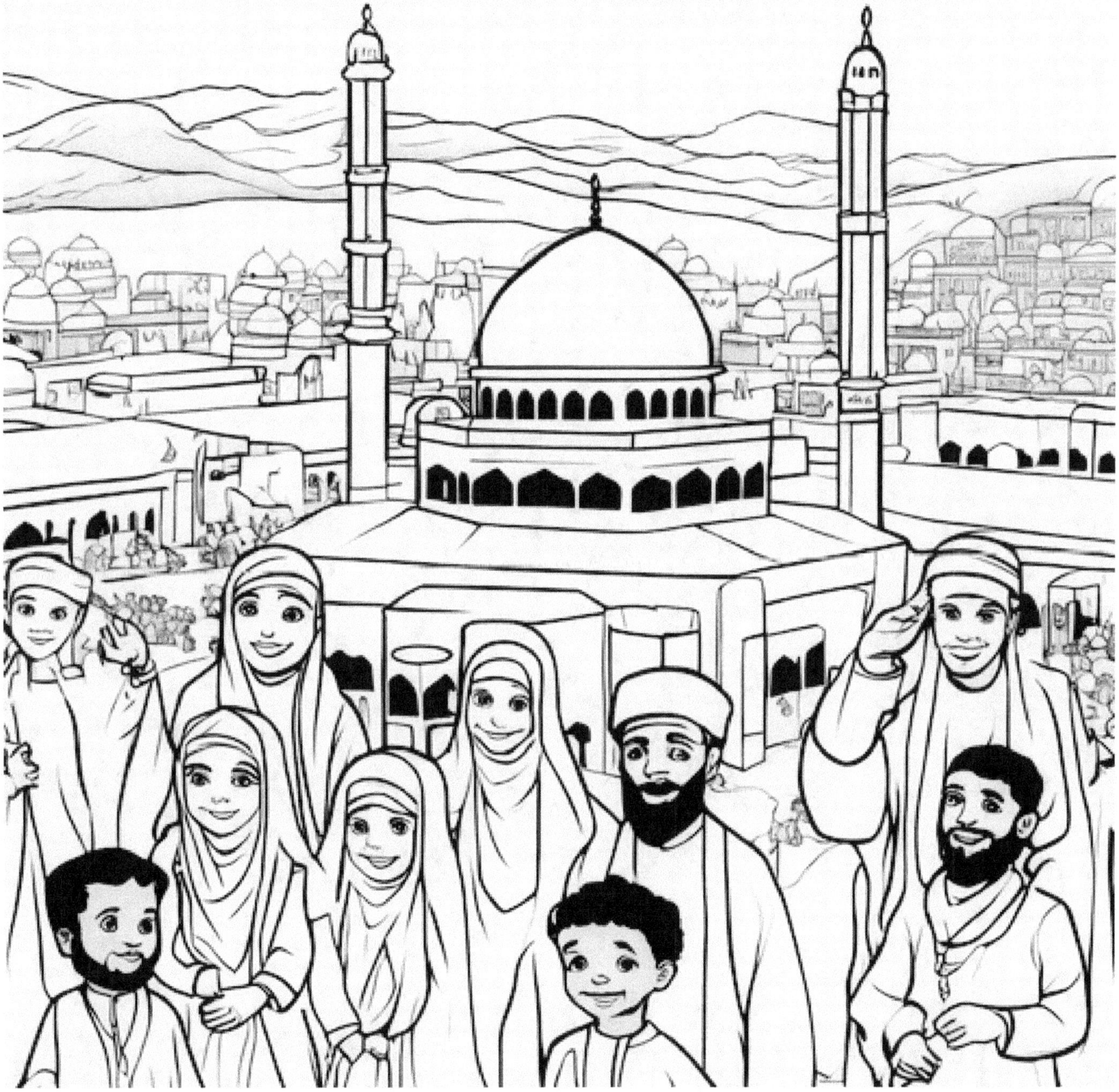

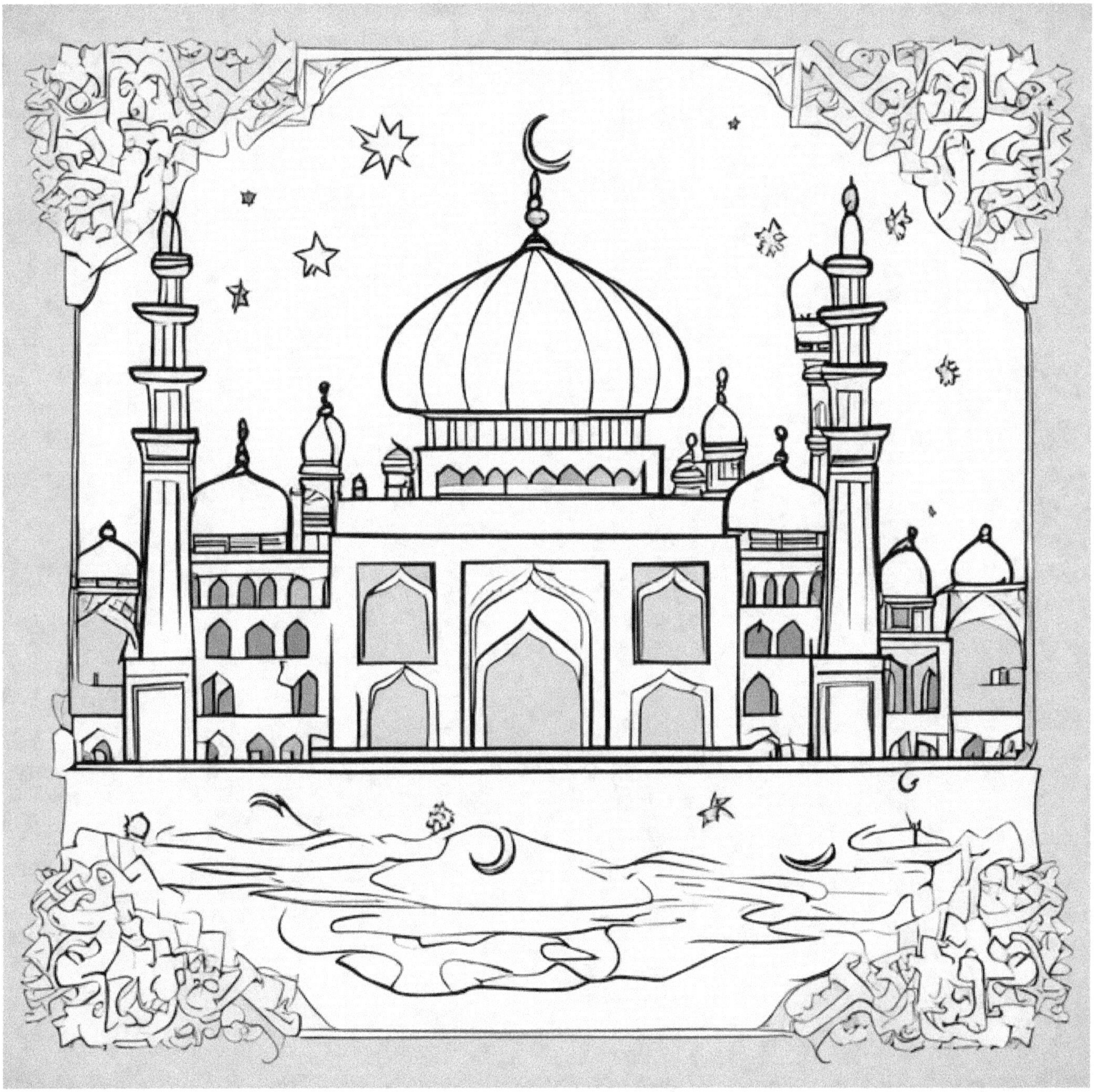

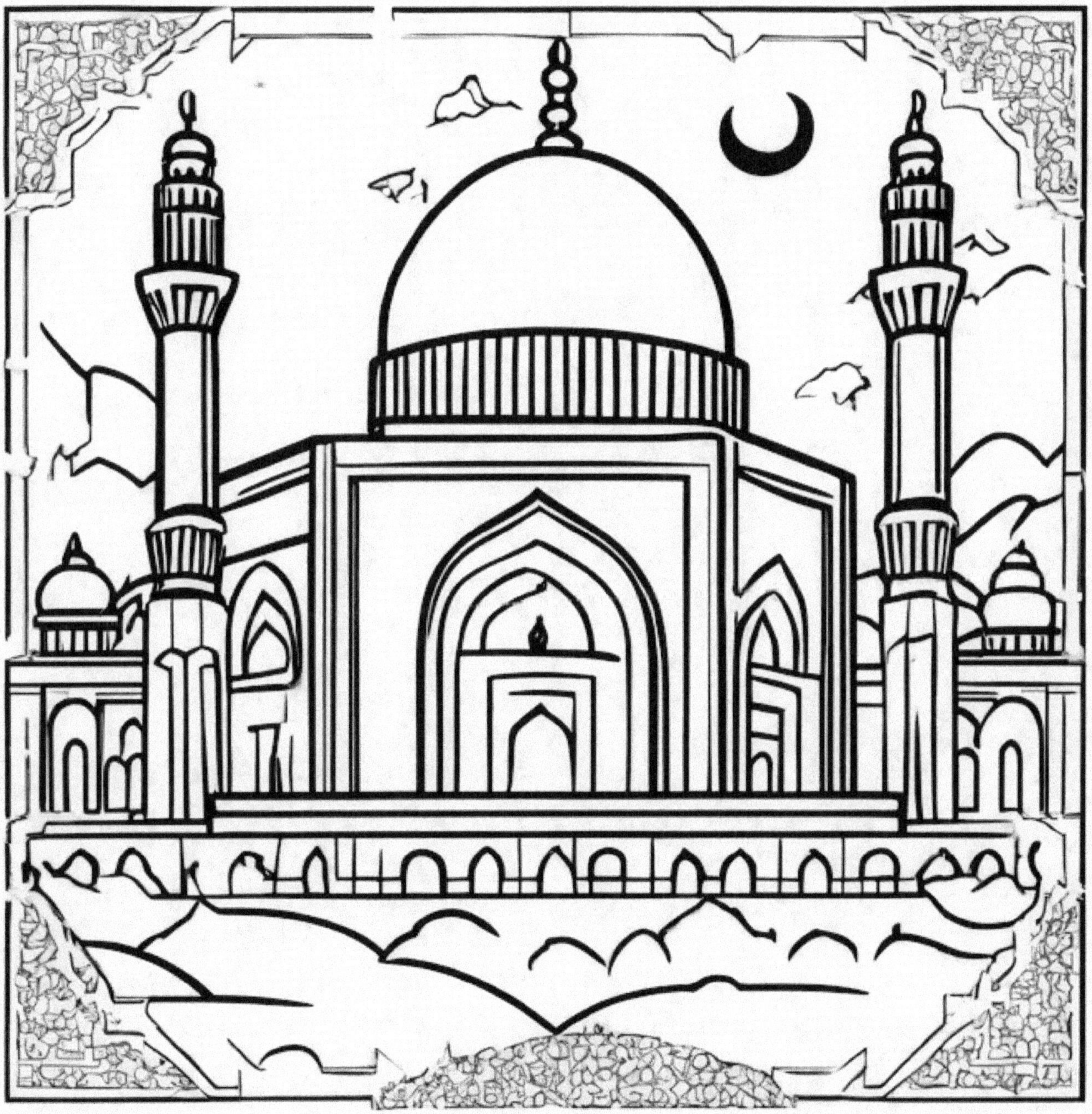

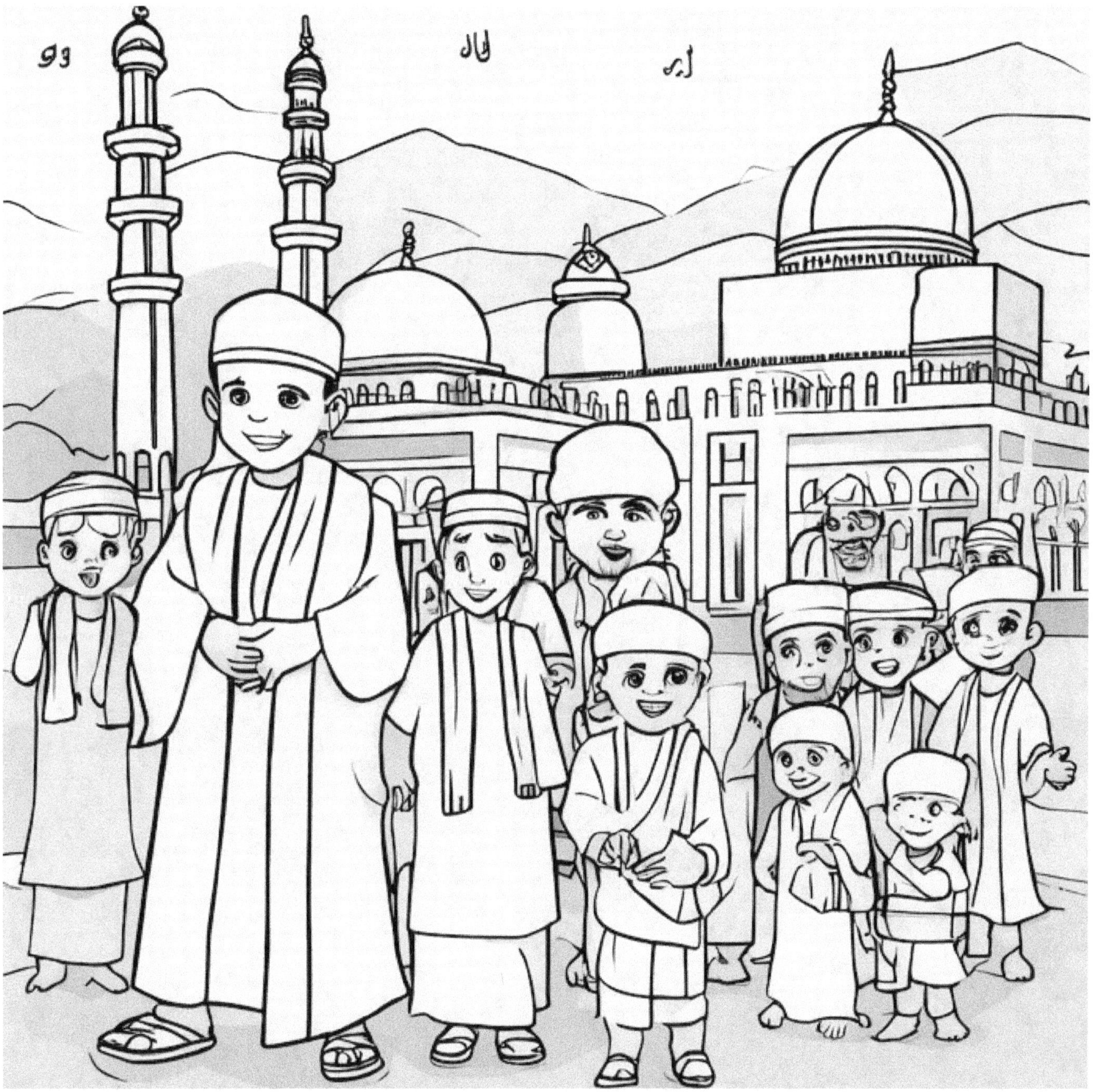

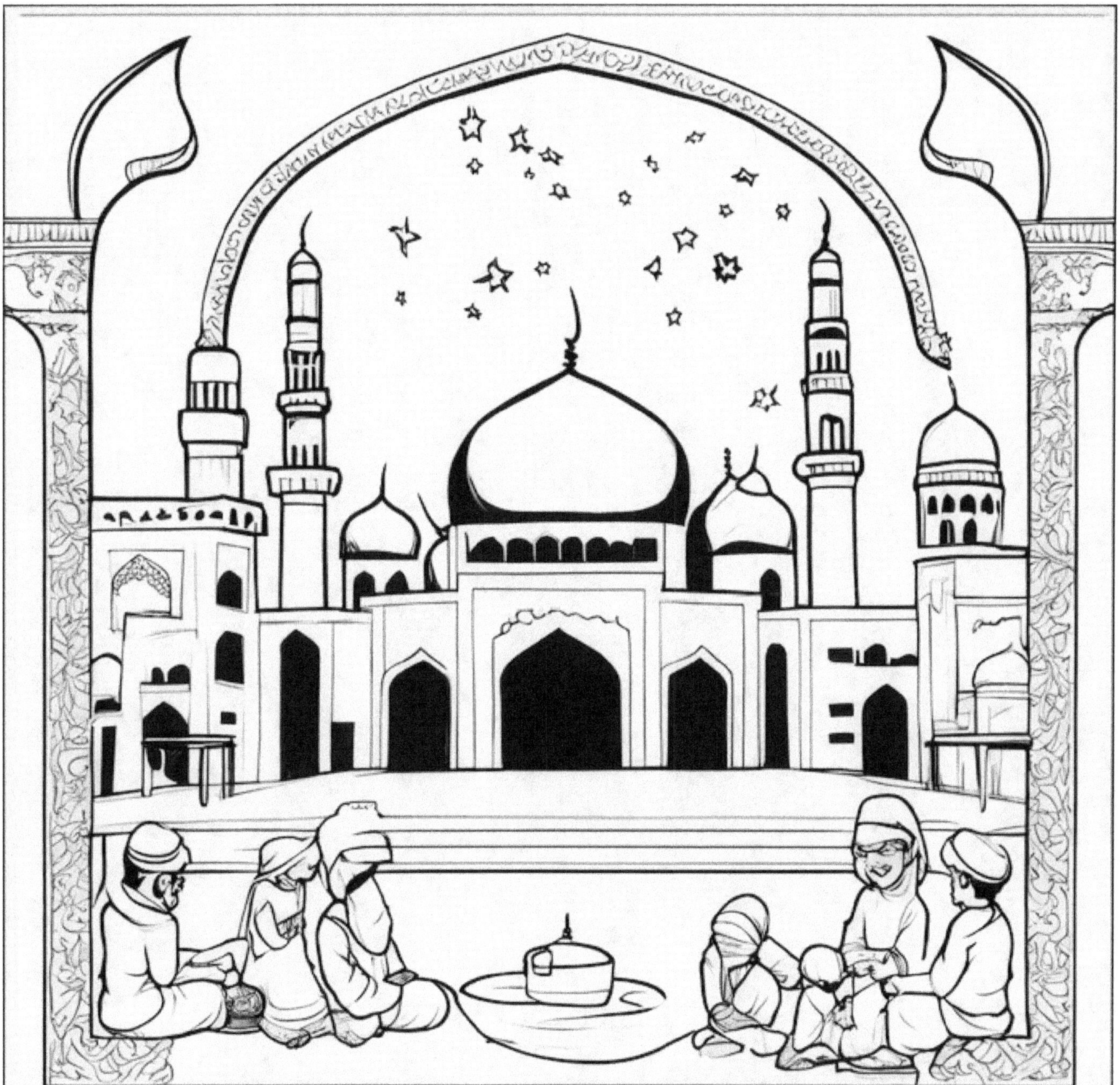

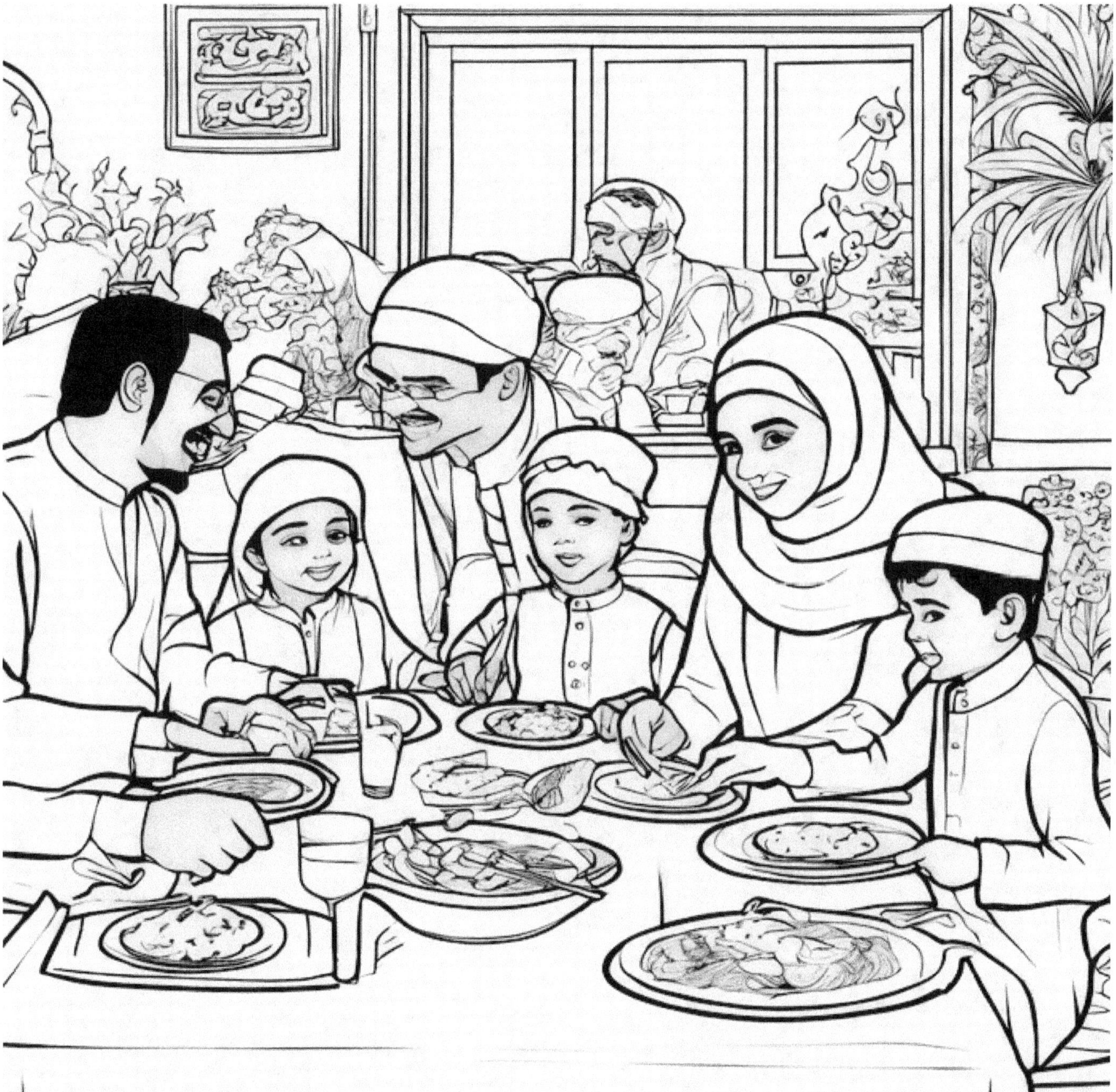

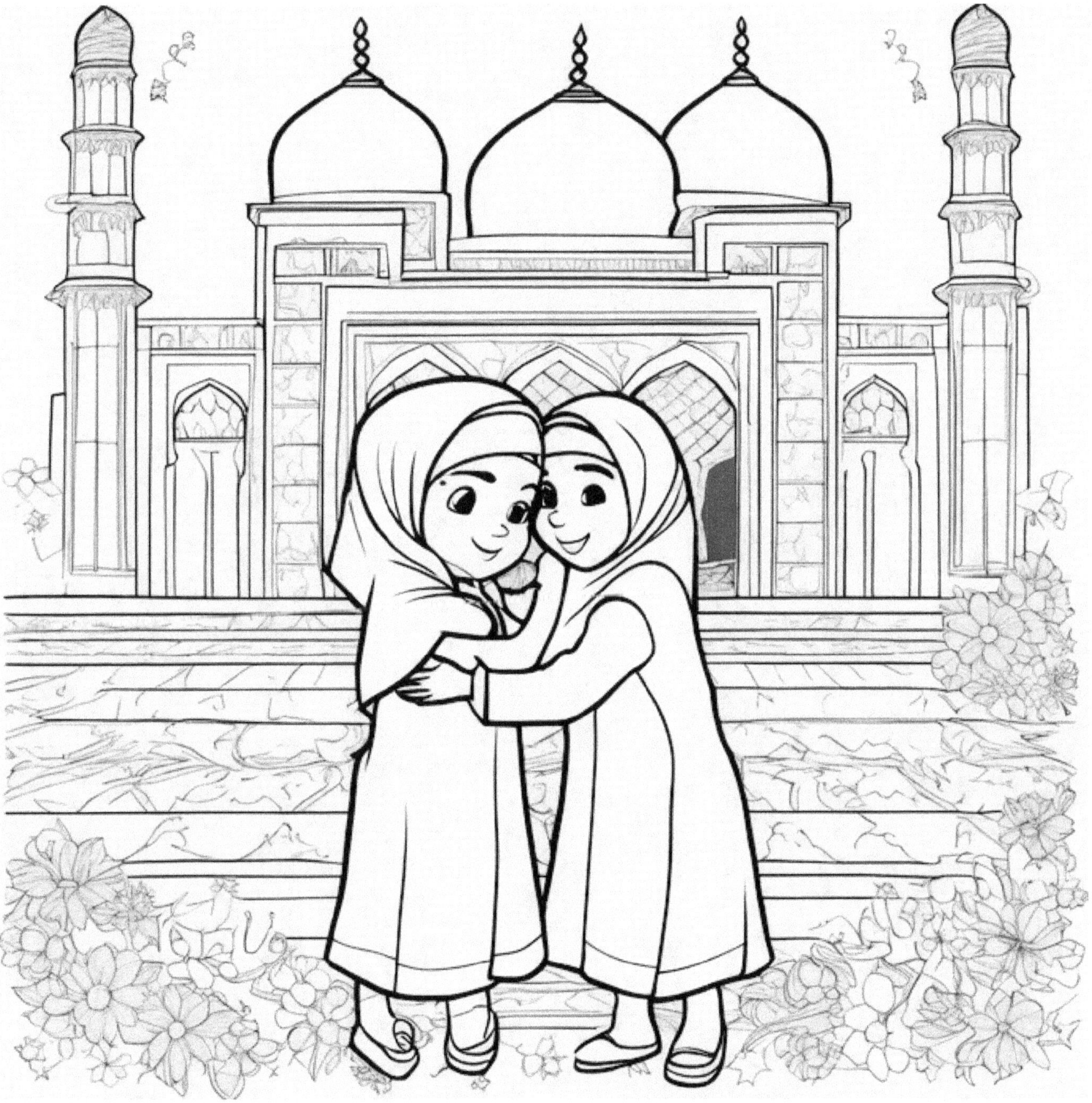

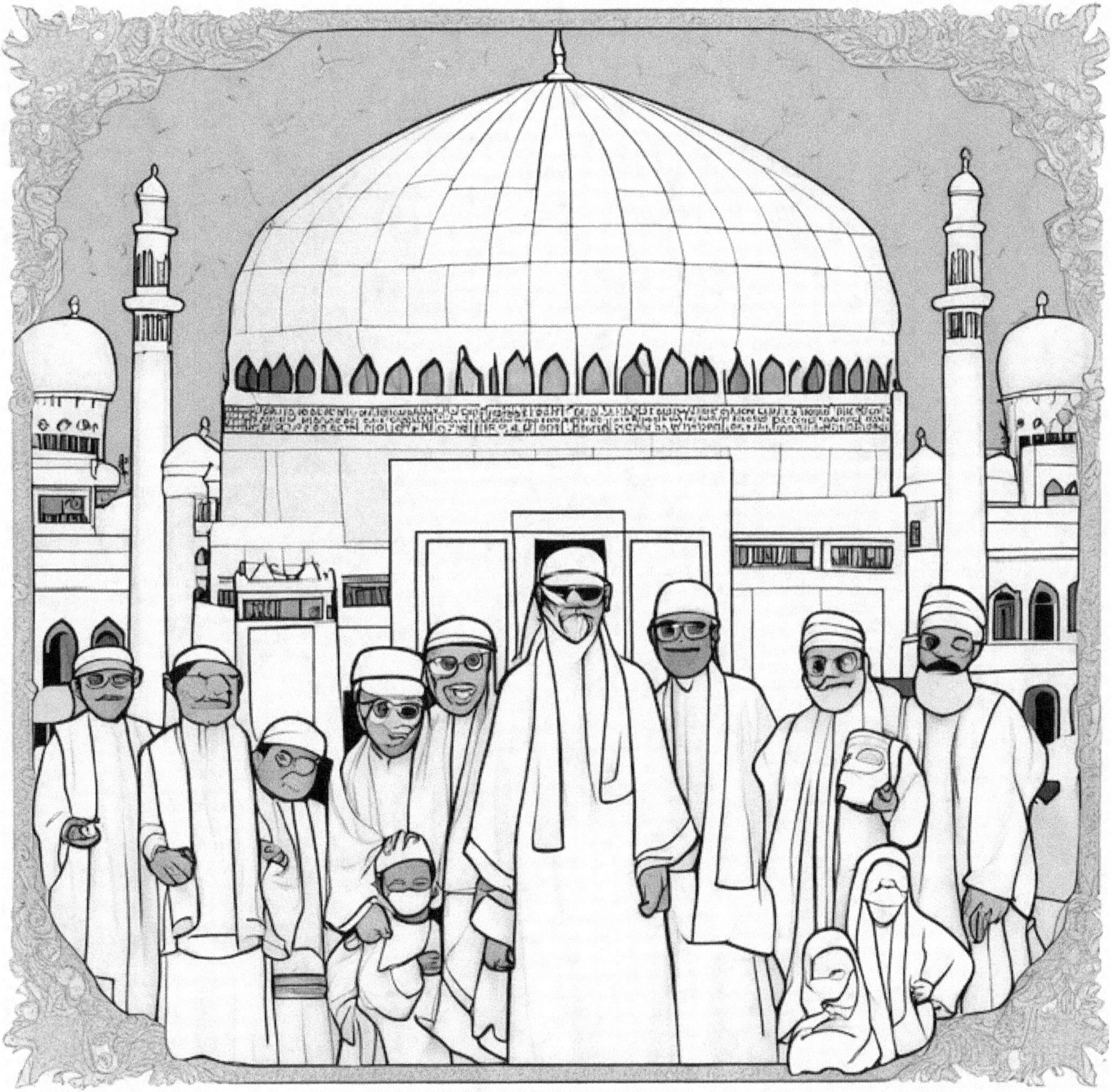

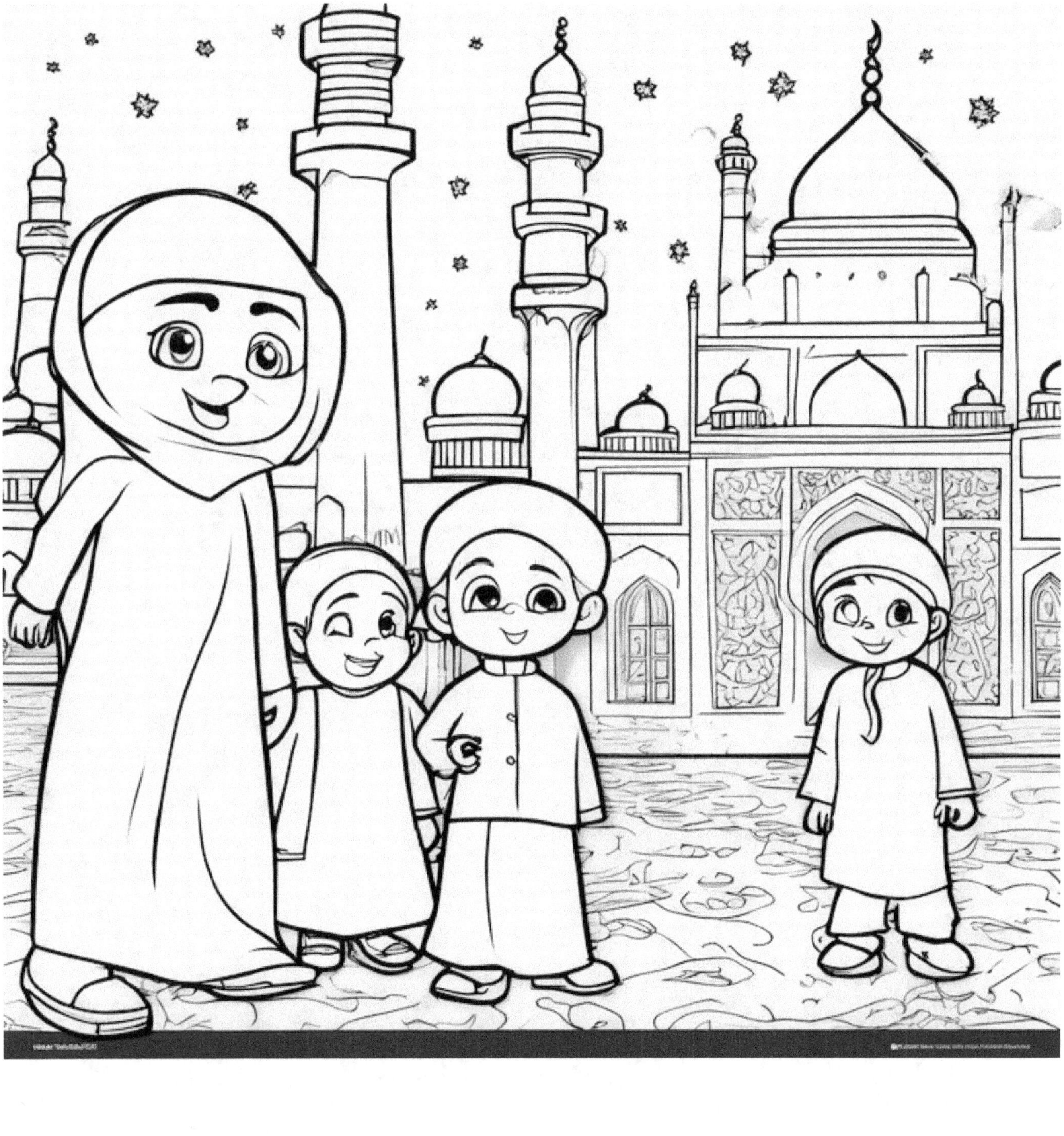

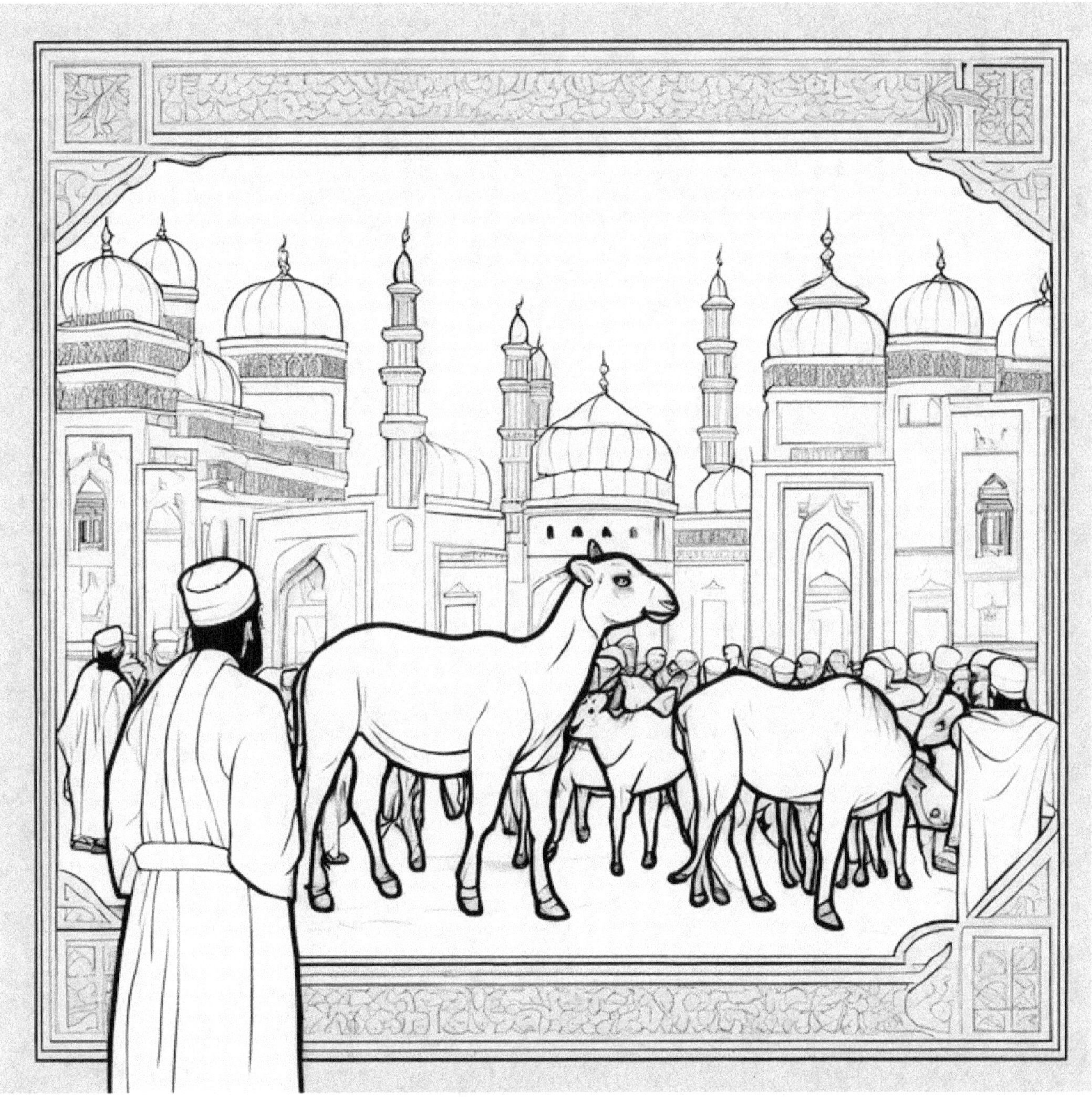

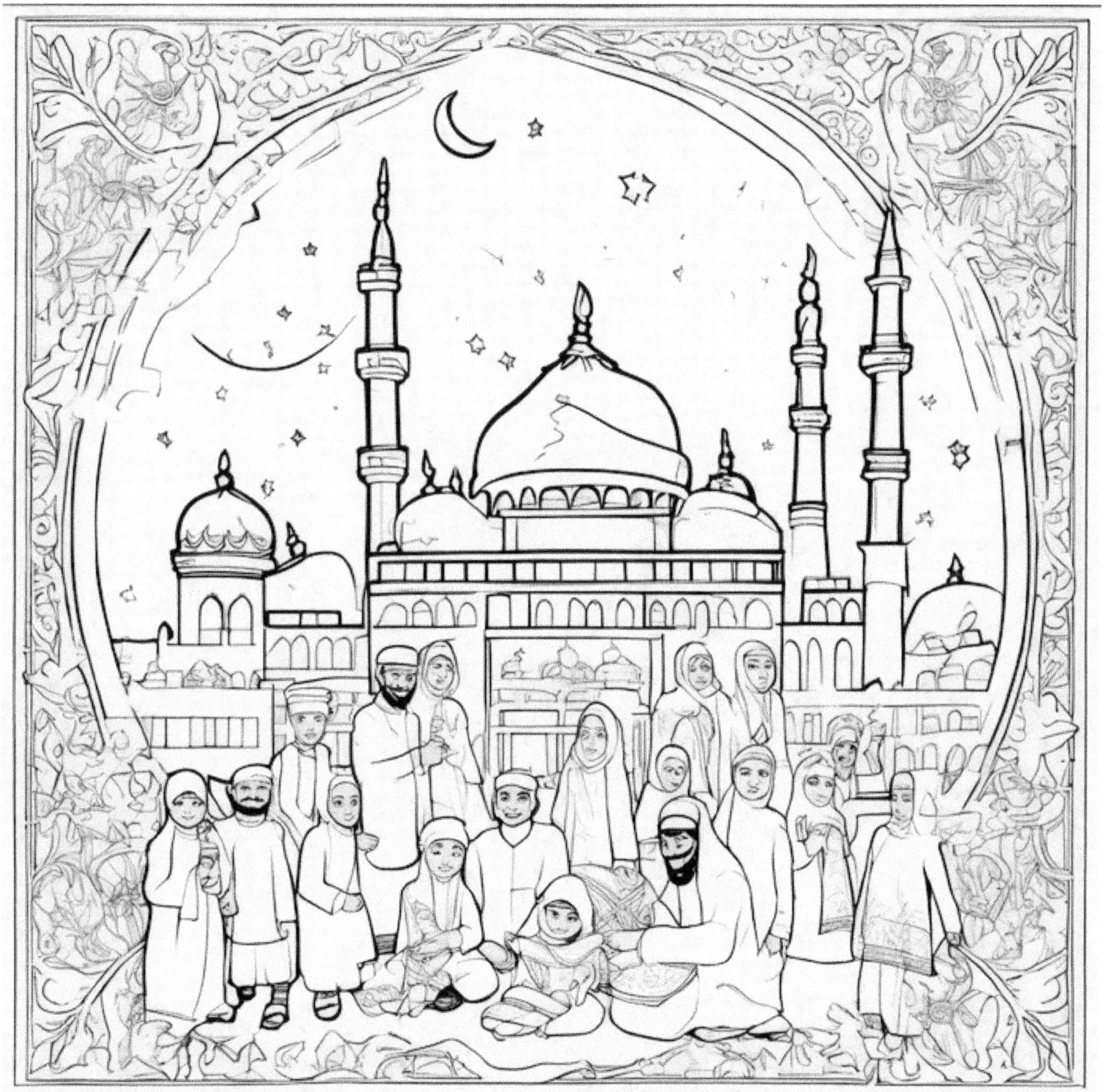

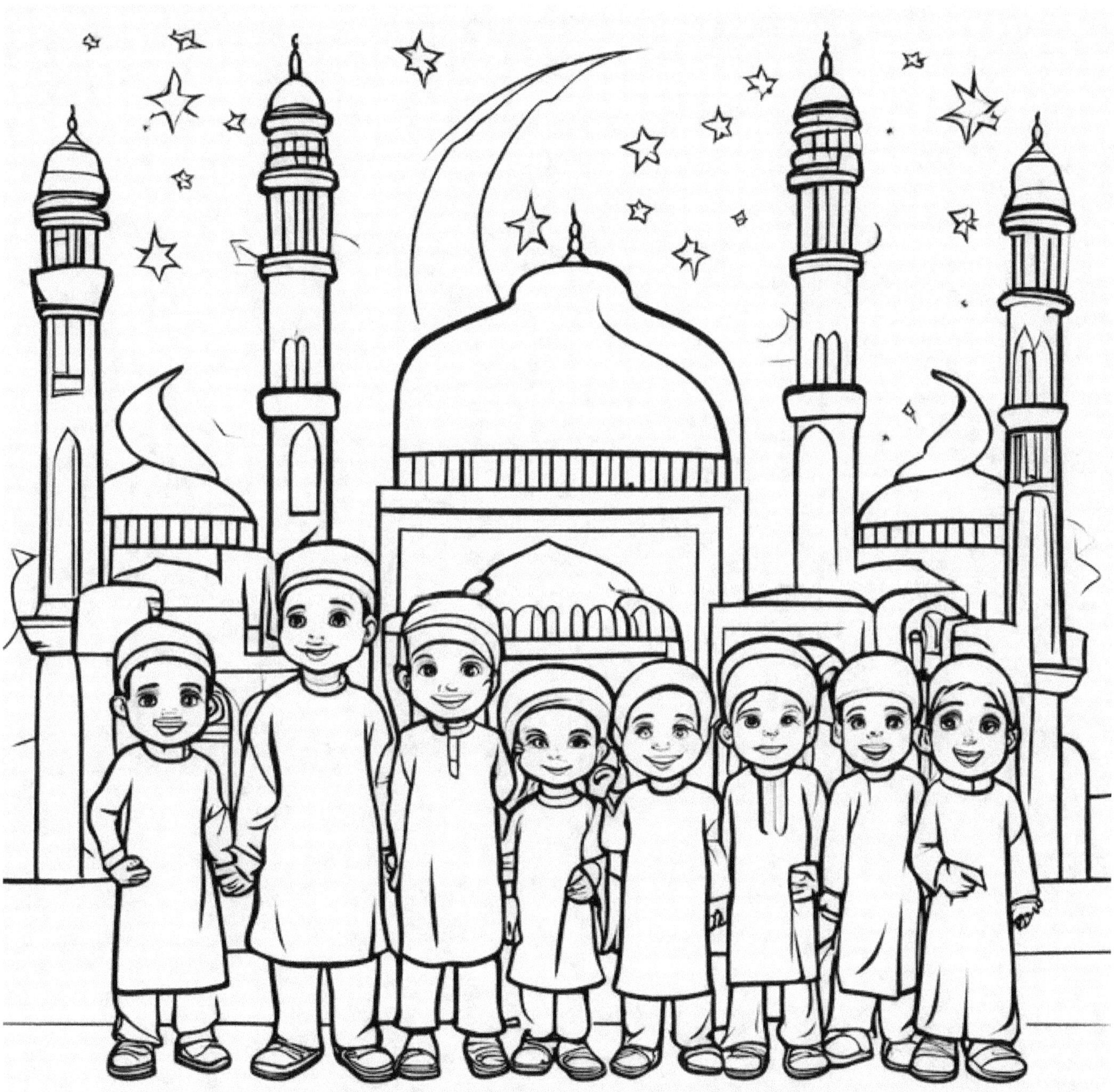

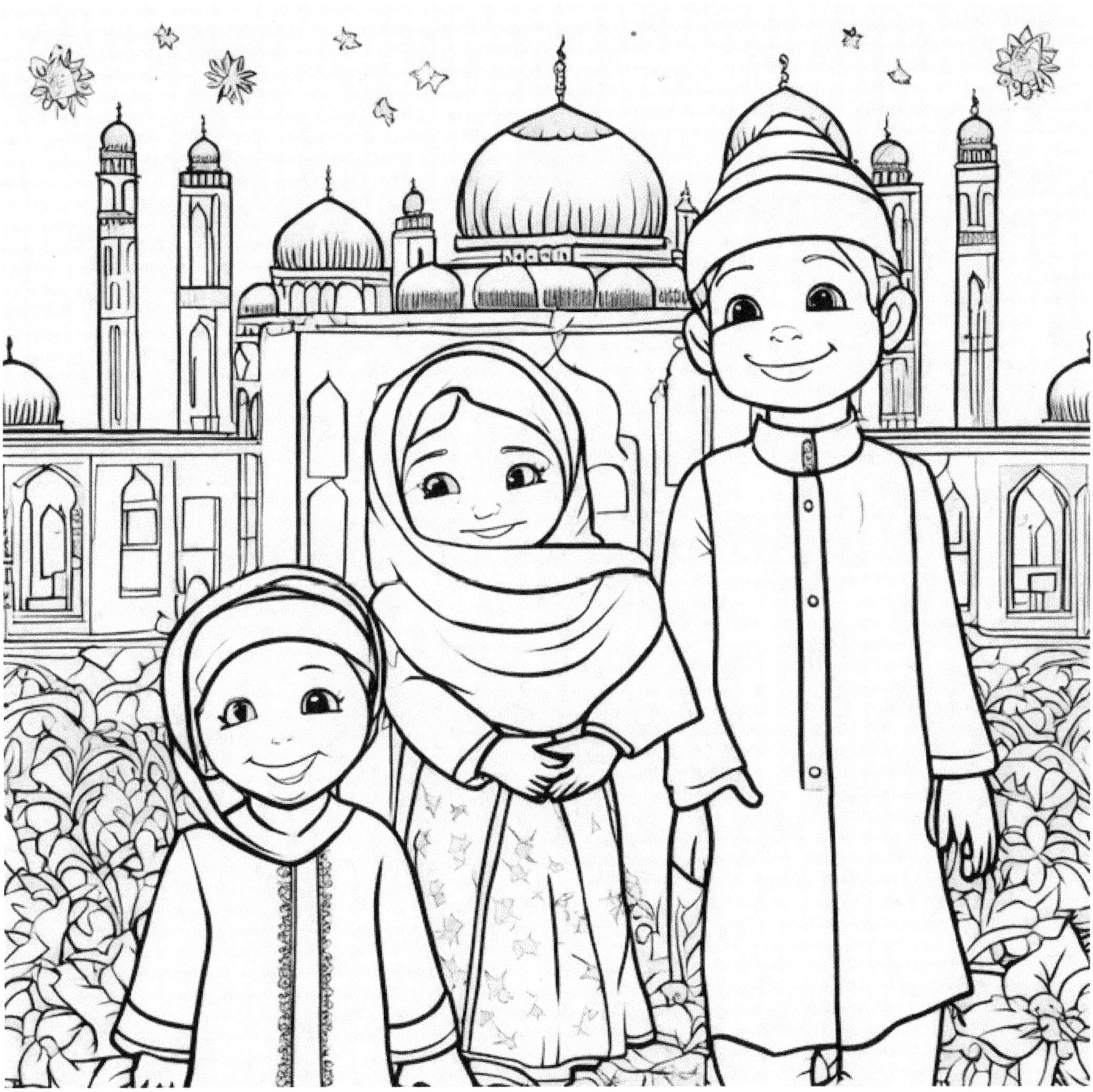

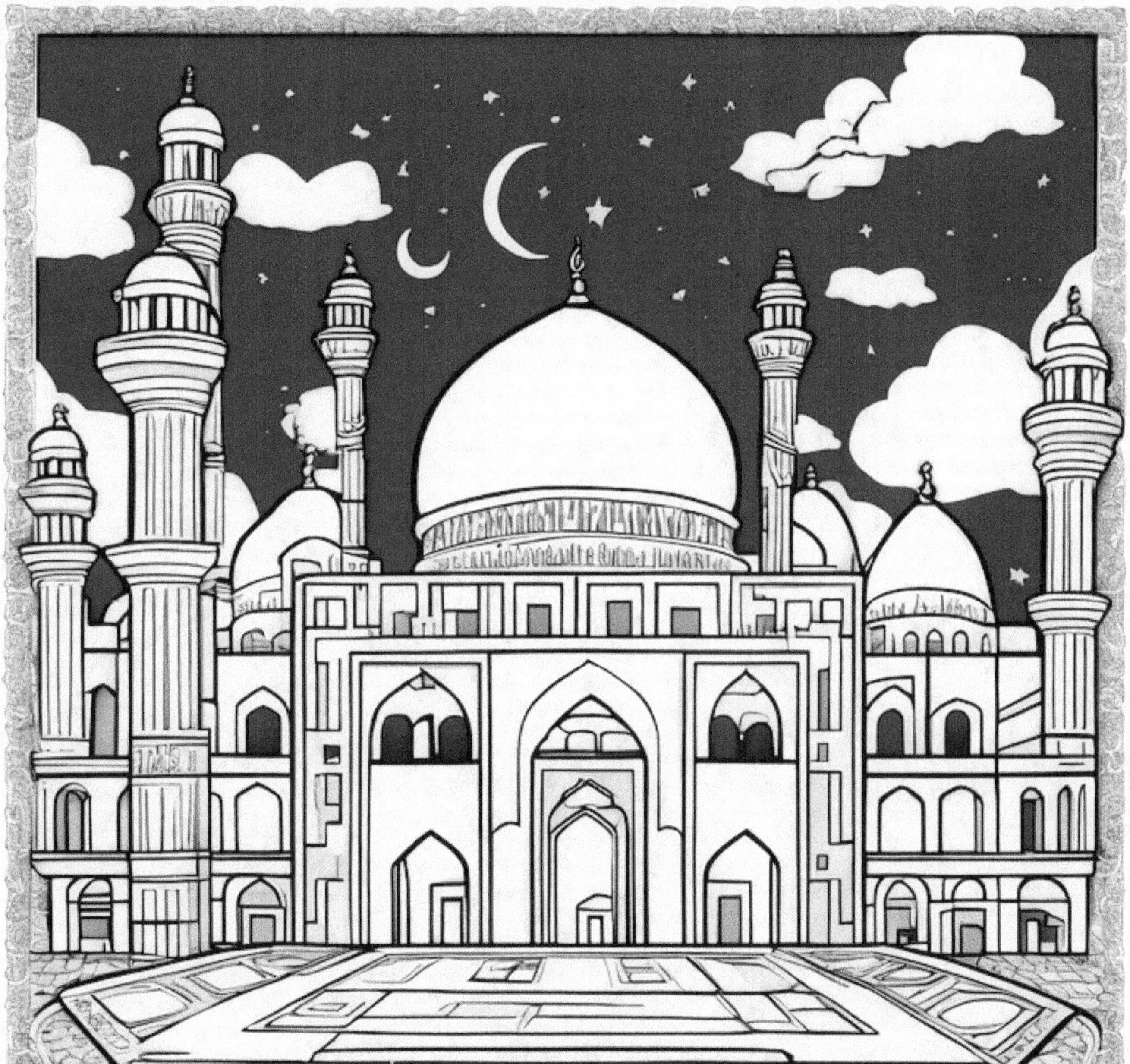

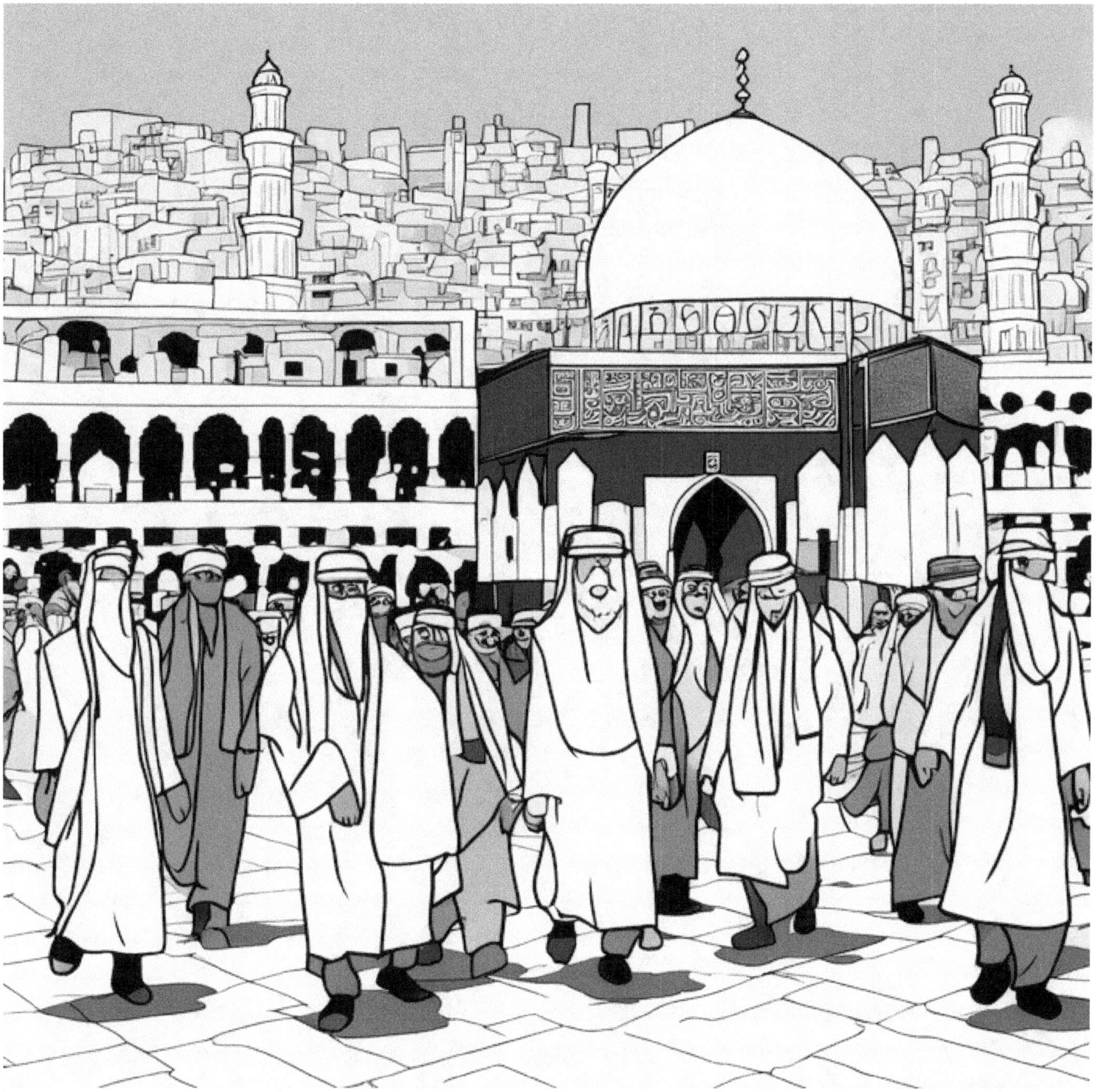

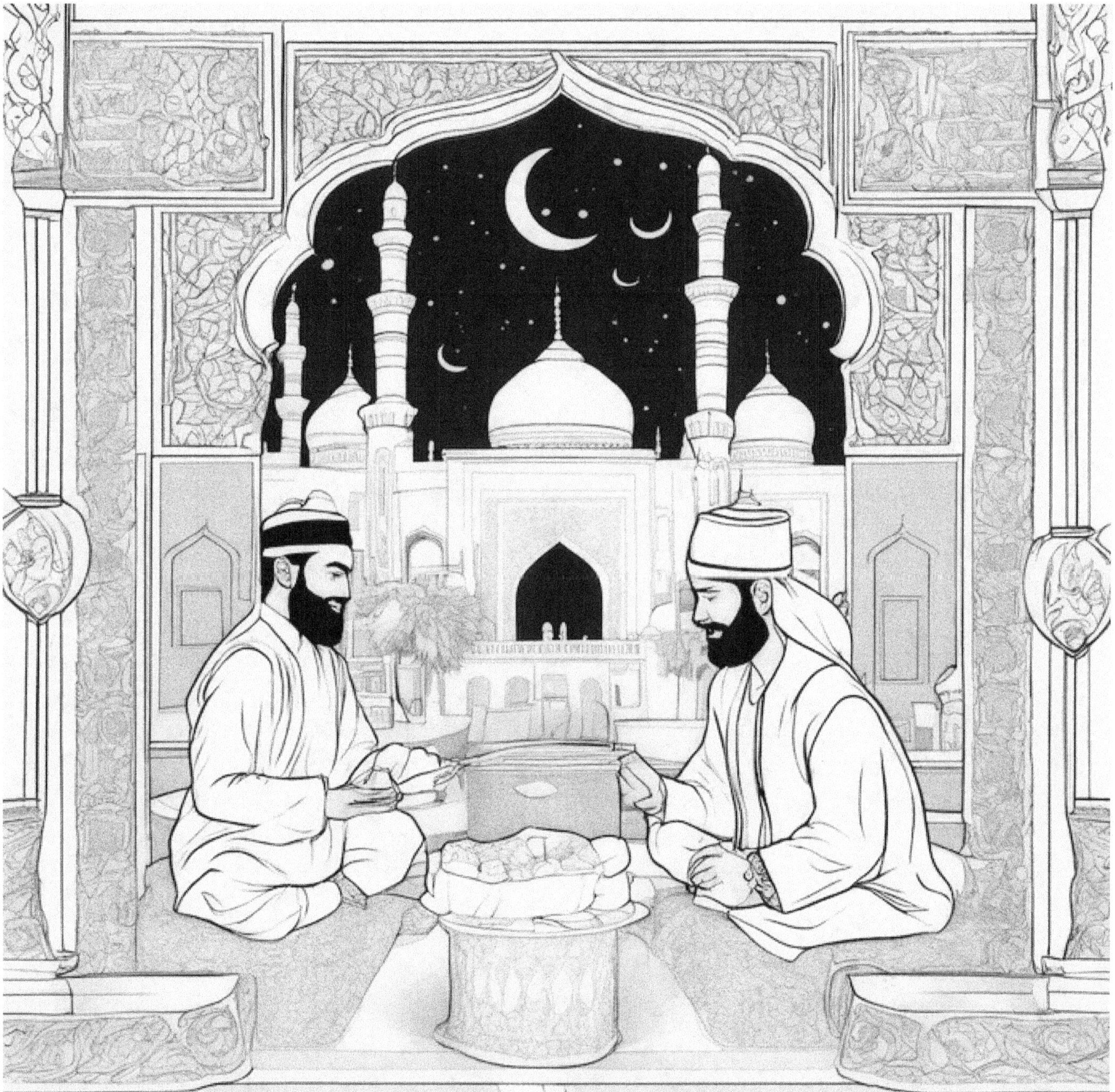

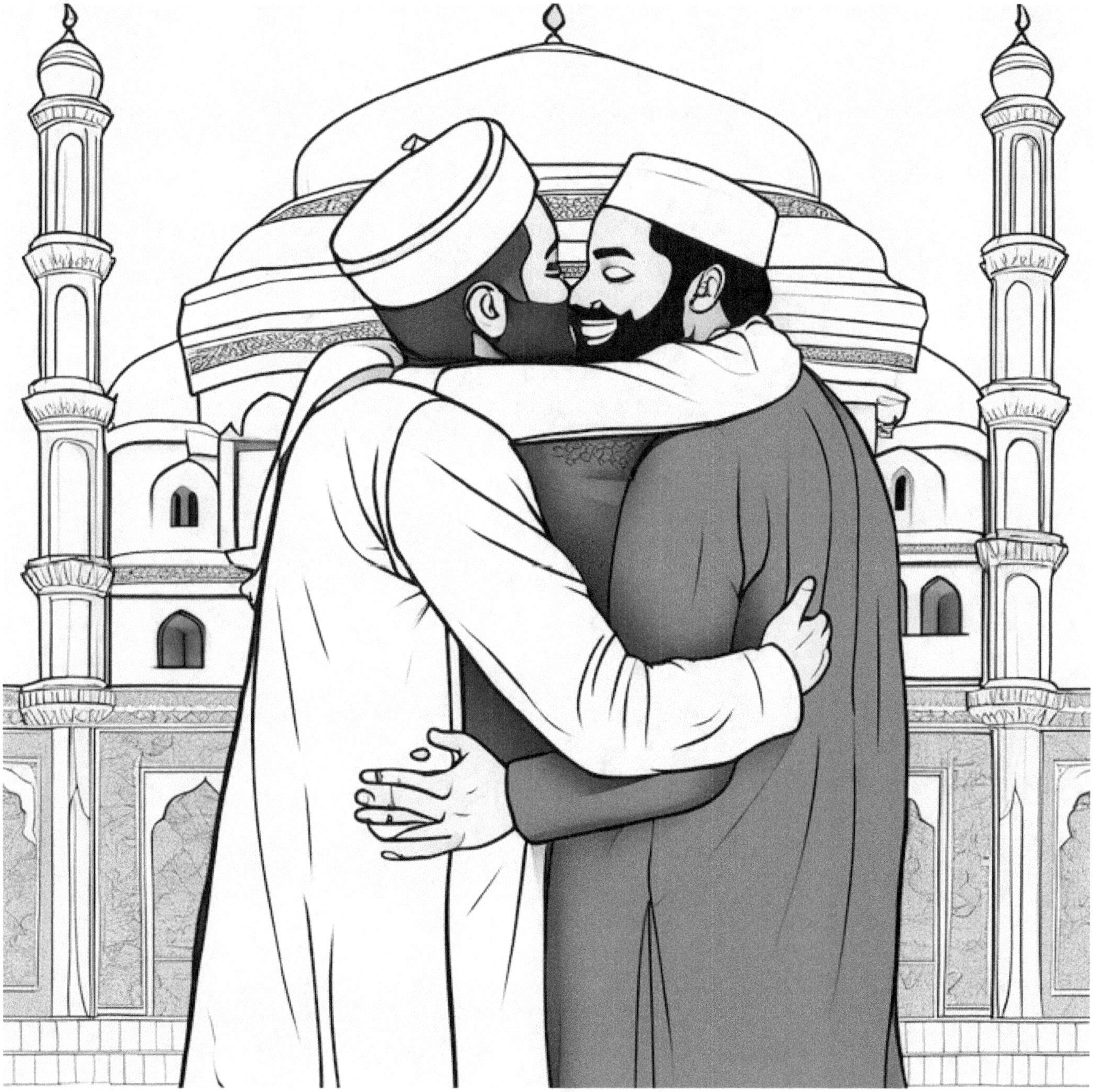

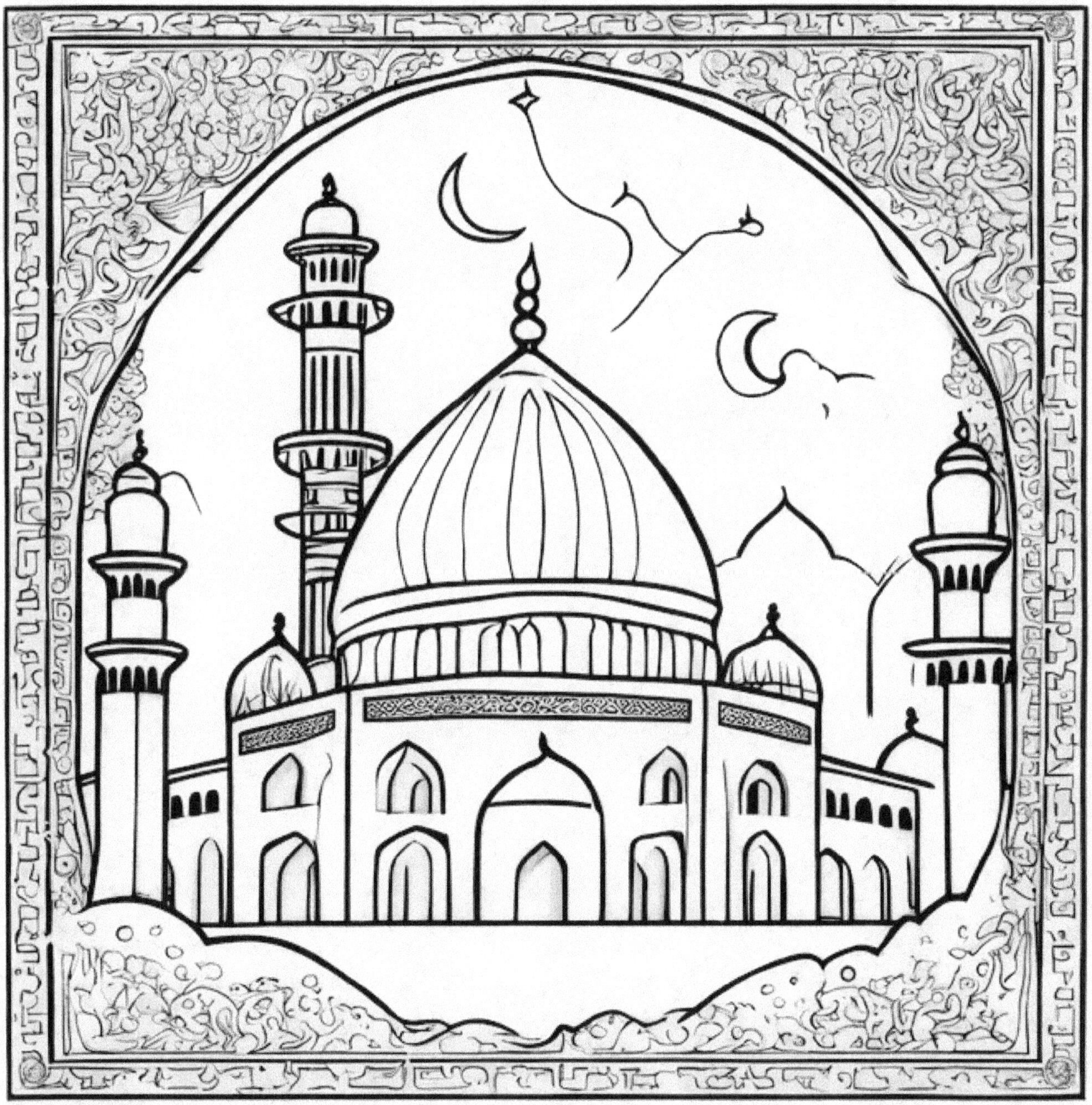

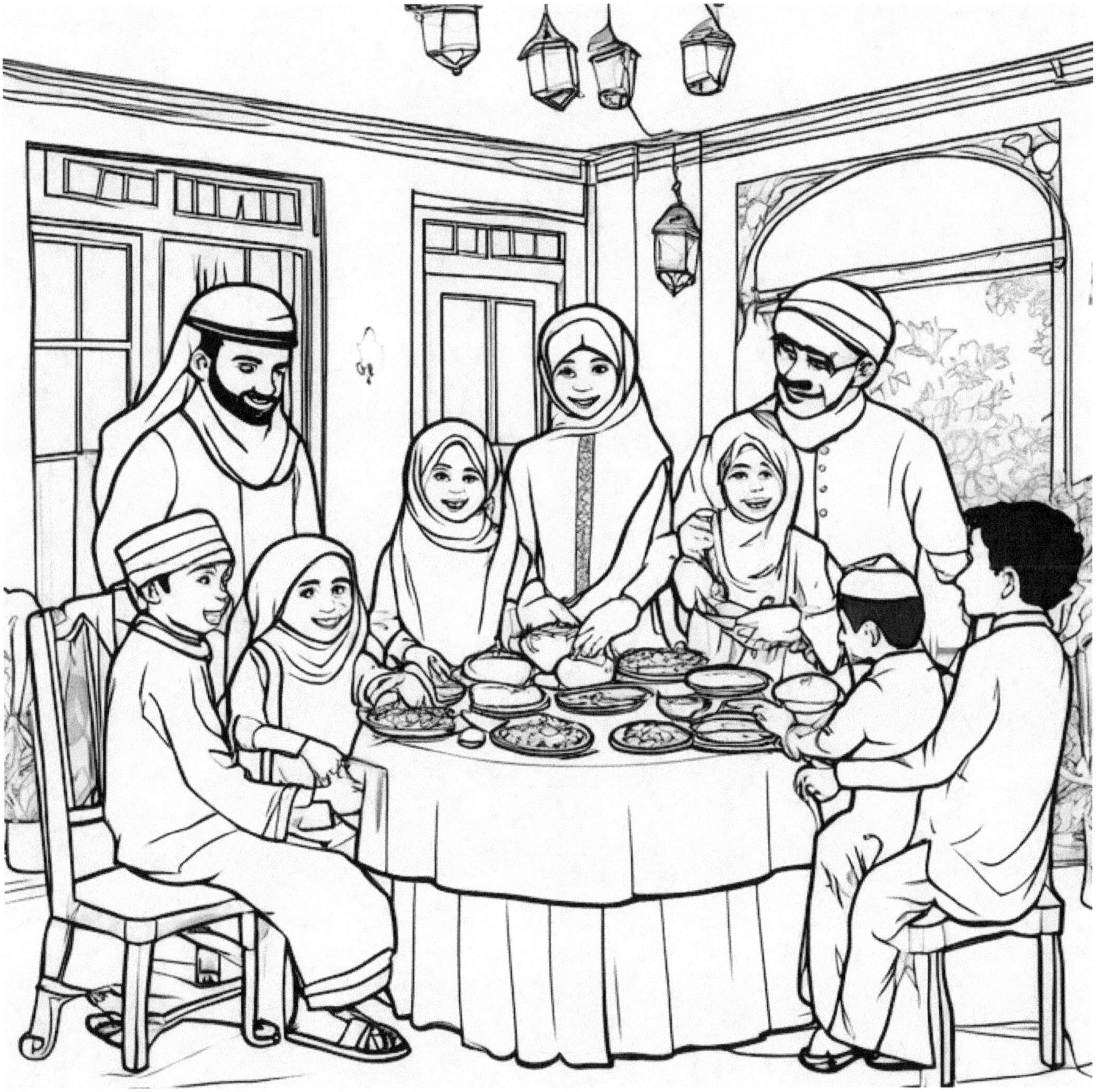

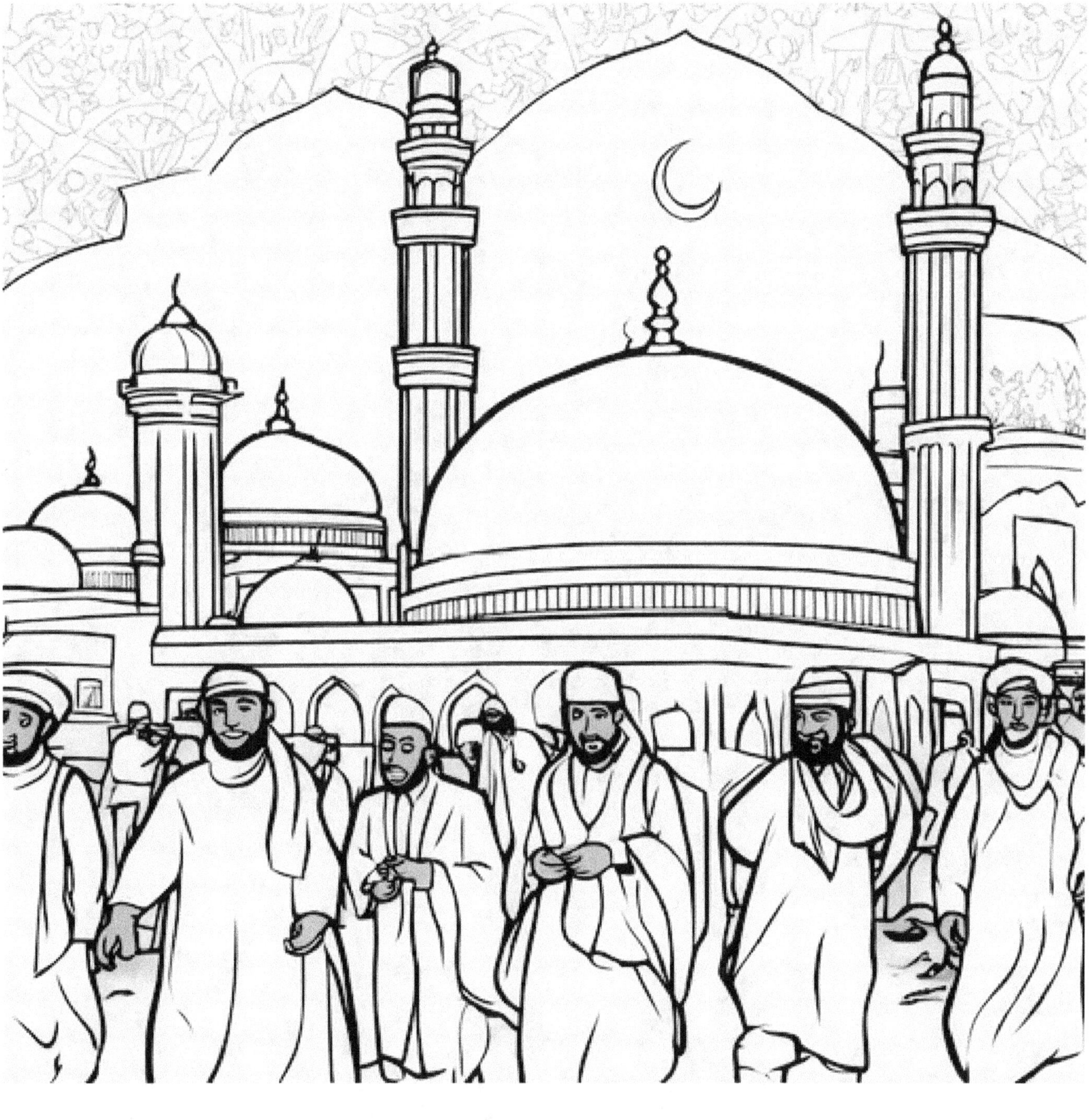

FIDY 4 ANMIA ED UL f Sarcies

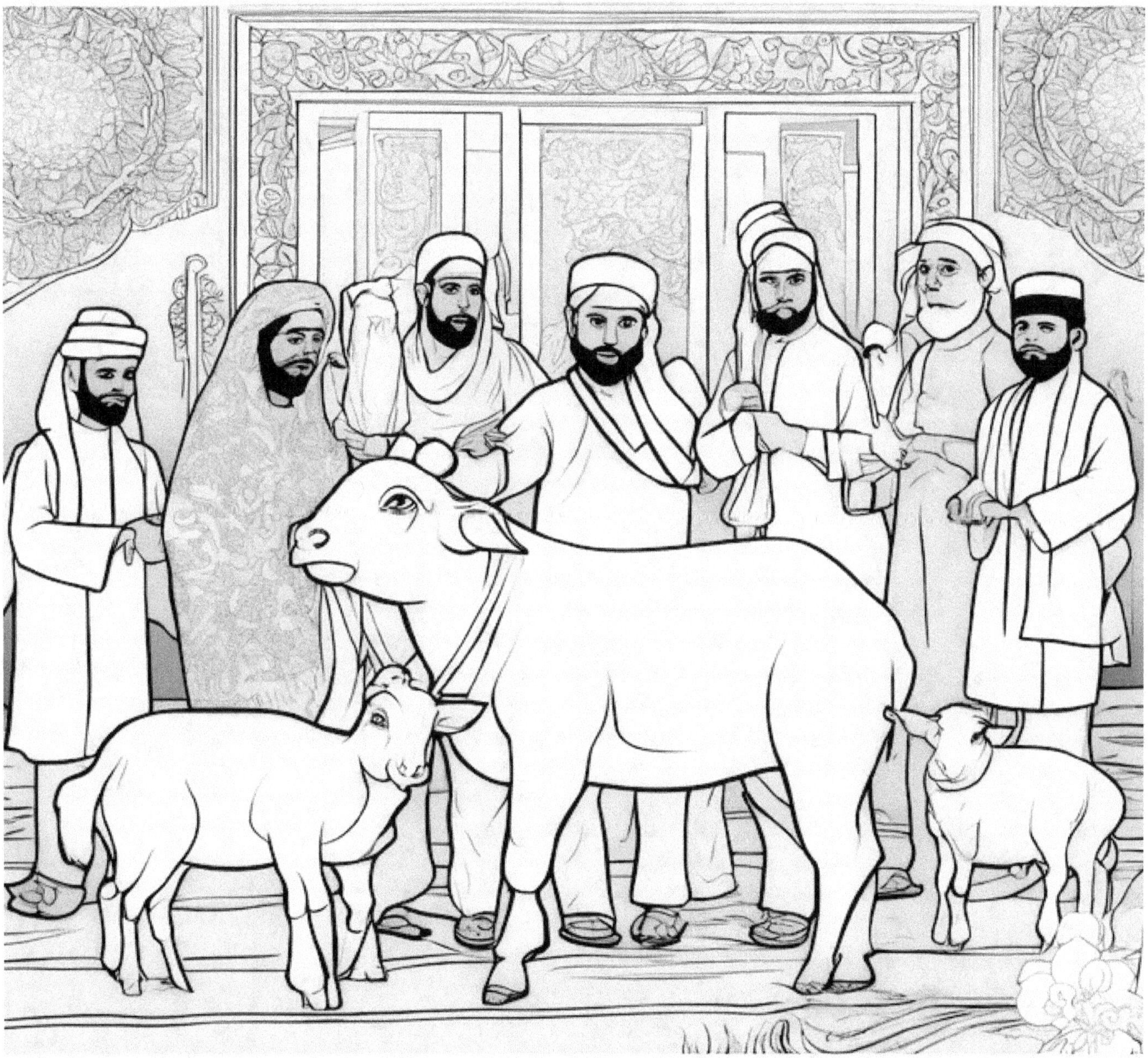

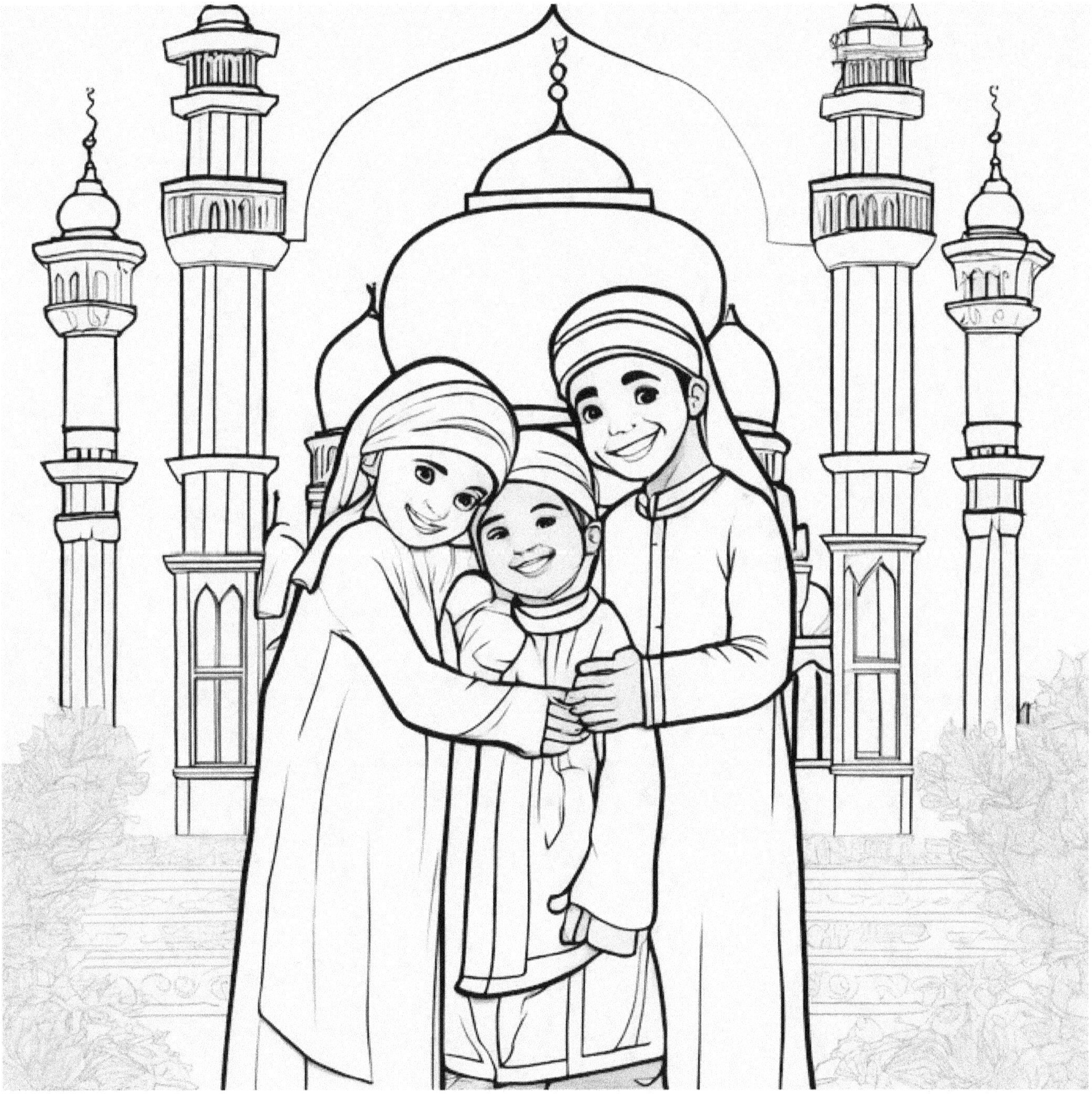

www.ingramcontent.com/pod-product-compliance
Lightning Source LLC
Chambersburg PA
CBHW082229290526
45794CB00009B/3735